MznLnx

Missing Links Exam Preps

Exam Prep for

Selling: Building Partnerships

Weitz, Castleberry, & Tanner, 6th Edition

The MznLnx Exam Prep is your link from the texbook and lecture to your exams.
The MznLnx Exam Preps are unauthorized and comprehensive reviews of your textbooks.

All material provided by MznLnx and Rico Publications (c) 2010
Textbook publishers and textbook authors do not particpate in or contribute to these reviews.

MznLnx

Rico Publications

Exam Prep for Selling: Building Partnerships
6th Edition
Weitz, Castleberry, & Tanner

Publisher: Raymond Houge
Assistant Editor: Michael Rouger
Text and Cover Designer: Lisa Buckner
Marketing Manager: Sara Swagger
Project Manager, Editorial Production: Jerry Emerson
Art Director: Vernon Lowerui

Product Manager: Dave Mason
Editorial Asitant: Rachel Guzmanji
Pedagogy: Debra Long
Cover Image: Jim Reed/Getty Images
Text and Cover Printer: City Printing, Inc.
Compositor: Media Mix, Inc.

(c) 2010 Rico Publications
ALL RIGHTS RESERVED. No part of this work covered by the copyright may be reproduced or used in any form or by an means--graphic, electronic, or mechanical, including photocopying, recording, taping, Web distribution, information storage, and retrieval systems, or in any other manner--without the written permission of the publisher.

Printed in the United States
ISBN:

For more information about our products, contact us at:
Dave.Mason@RicoPublications.com

For permission to use material from this text or product, submit a request online to:
Dave.Mason@RicoPublications.com

Contents

CHAPTER 1
Selling and Salespeople — 1

CHAPTER 2
Building Partnering Relationships — 7

CHAPTER 3
Ethical and Legal Issues in Selling — 12

CHAPTER 4
Buying Behavior and the Buying Process — 17

CHAPTER 5
Using Communication Principles to Build Relationships — 23

CHAPTER 6
Adaptive Selling for Relationship Building — 27

CHAPTER 7
Prospecting — 28

CHAPTER 8
Planning the Sales Call — 33

CHAPTER 9
Making the Sales Call — 35

CHAPTER 10
Strengthening the Presentation — 37

CHAPTER 11
Responding to Objections — 43

CHAPTER 12
Obtaining Commitment — 44

CHAPTER 13
Formal Negotiating — 45

CHAPTER 14
After the Sale: Building Long-Term Partnerships — 46

CHAPTER 15
Managing Your Time and Territory — 48

CHAPTER 16
Managing within Your Company — 50

CHAPTER 17
Managing Your Career — 54

ANSWER KEY — 55

TO THE STUDENT

COMPREHENSIVE

The *MznLnx* Exam Prep series is designed to help you pass your exams. Editors at MznLnx review your textbooks and then prepare these practice exams to help you master the textbook material. Unlike study guides, workbooks, and practice tests provided by the texbook publisher and textbook authors, *MznLnx* gives you **all** of the material in each chapter in exam form, not just samples, so you can be sure to nail your exam.

MECHANICAL

The MznLnx Exam Prep series creates exams that will help you learn the subject matter as well as test you on your understanding. Each question is designed to help you master the concept. Just working through the exams, you gain an understanding of the subject--its a simple mechanical process that produces success.

INTEGRATED STUDY GUIDE AND REVIEW

MznLnx is not just a set of exams designed to test you, its also a comprehensive review of the subject content. Each exam question is also a review of the concept, making sure that you will get the answer correct without having to go to other sources of material. You learn as you go! Its the easiest way to pass an exam.

HUMOR

Studying can be tedious and dry. MznLnx's instructional design includes moderate humor within the exam questions on occassion, to break the tedium and revitalize the brain

Chapter 1. Selling and Salespeople

1. A _____ is a type of business entity in which partners (owners) share with each other the profits or losses of the business undertaking in which all have invested. _____s are often favored over corporations for taxation purposes, as the _____ structure does not generally incur a tax on profits before it is distributed to the partners (i.e. there is no dividend tax levied.) However, depending on the _____ structure and the jurisdiction in which it operates, owners of a _____ may be exposed to greater personal liability than they would as shareholders of a corporation.
    a. Partnership
    b. Brand piracy
    c. Fair Debt Collection Practices Act
    d. Competition law

2. _____ is an advertisement in which a particular product specifically mentions a competitor by name for the express purpose of showing why the competitor is inferior to the product naming it.

    This should not be confused with parody advertisements, where a fictional product is being advertised for the purpose of poking fun at the particular advertisement, nor should it be confused with the use of a coined brand name for the purpose of comparing the product without actually naming an actual competitor. ('Wikipedia tastes better and is less filling than the Encyclopedia Galactica.')

    In the 1980s, during what has been referred to as the cola wars, soft-drink manufacturer Pepsi ran a series of advertisements where people, caught on hidden camera, in a blind taste test, chose Pepsi over rival Coca-Cola.

    a. GL-70
    b. Cost per conversion
    c. Comparative advertising
    d. Heavy-up

3. A personal and cultural _____ is a relative ethic _____, an assumption upon which implementation can be extrapolated. A _____ system is a set of consistent _____s and measures that is soo not true. A principle _____ is a foundation upon which other _____s and measures of integrity are based.
    a. Package-on-Package
    b. Supreme Court of the United States
    c. Perceptual maps
    d. Value

4. In the field of marketing, a customer _____ consists of the sum total of benefits which a vendor promises that a customer will receive in return for the customer's associated payment (or other value-transfer.)

    Put simply, the _____ is what the customer gets for his money.

Accordingly, a customer can evaluate a company's value-proposition on two broad dimensions with multiple subsets:

1. relative performance: what the customer gets from the vendor relative to a competitor's offering;
2. price: which consists of the payment the customer makes to acquire the product or service; plus the access cost

The vendor-company's marketing and sales efforts offer a customer _____; the vendor-company's delivery and customer-service processes then fulfill that value-proposition.

A value-proposition can assist in a firm's marketing strategy, and may guide a business to target a particular market segment.

   a. DefCom Australia
   b. Marketing performance measurement and management
   c. Relationship management
   d. Value proposition

5. In Marketing Management, _____ strategy encompasses the channels that a company uses to connect with its customers/business and the organizational processes it develops (such as high tech product development) to guide customer interactions from initial contact through fulfilment.

A firm _____ is the delivery mechanism for their unique value proposition. That value proposition is based on the choices the business has made to focus on and invest in markets and solutions that they believe will respond positively to the increased attention.

   a. Gold Key Matching Service
   b. Go-to-market
   c. Net Promoter[R] score
   d. Better Living Through Chemistry

6. In marketing, customer _____, lifetime customer value (LCV), or _____ (LTV) and a new concept of 'customer life cycle management' is the present value of the future cash flows attributed to the customer relationship. Use of customer _____ as a marketing metric tends to place greater emphasis on customer service and long-term customer satisfaction, rather than on maximizing short-term sales.

Customer _____ has intuitive appeal as a marketing concept, because in theory it represents exactly how much each customer is worth in monetary terms, and therefore exactly how much a marketing department should be willing to spend to acquire each customer.

a. Sweepstakes
b. Value chain
c. Brand infiltration
d. Lifetime value

7. _____ is the practice of individuals including commercial businesses, governments and institutions, facilitating the sale of their products or services to other companies or organizations that in turn resell them, use them as components in products or services they offer _____ is also called business-to-_____ for short. (Note that while marketing to government entities shares some of the same dynamics of organizational marketing, B2G Marketing is meaningfully different.)

a. Law of disruption
b. Mass marketing
c. Disruptive technology
d. Business marketing

8. A _____ is a plan of action designed to achieve a particular goal.

_____ is different from tactics. In military terms, tactics is concerned with the conduct of an engagement while _____ is concerned with how different engagements are linked.

a. 6-3-5 Brainwriting
b. Power III
c. 180SearchAssistant
d. Strategy

9. _____ , according to The American Marketing Association, is 'a planning process designed to assure that all brand contacts received by a customer or prospect for a product, service, or organization are relevant to that person and consistent over time.' (Marketing Power Dictionary)

_____ is a term used to describe a holistic approach to marketing. It aims to ensure consistency of message and the complementary use of media. The concept includes online and offline marketing channels.

a. ADTECH
b. AMAX
c. ACNielsen
d. Integrated marketing communications

10. _____ is defined by the American _____ Association as the activity, set of institutions, and processes for creating, communicating, delivering, and exchanging offerings that have value for customers, clients, partners, and society at large. The term developed from the original meaning which referred literally to going to market, as in shopping, or going to a market to sell goods or services.

_____ practice tends to be seen as a creative industry, which includes advertising, distribution and selling.

a. Product naming
b. Customer acquisition management
c. Marketing myopia
d. Marketing

11. _____ refers to messages and related media used to communicate with a market. Those who practice advertising, branding, direct marketing, graphic design, marketing, packaging, promotion, publicity, sponsorship, public relations, sales, sales promotion and online marketing are termed marketing communicators, _____ managers, or more briefly as marcom managers.

a. Merchandise
b. Sales promotion
c. Merchandising
d. Marketing communication

12. _____ in economics and business is the result of an exchange and from that trade we assign a numerical monetary value to a good, service or asset. If I trade 4 apples for an orange, the _____ of an orange is 4 - apples. Inversely, the _____ of an apple is 1/4 oranges.

a. Price
b. Discounts and allowances
c. Contribution margin-based pricing
d. Pricing

13. _____ is a term commonly used to describe commerce transactions between businesses like the one between a manufacturer and a wholesaler or a wholesaler and a retailer i.e both the buyer and the seller are business entity.This is unlike business-to-consumers (B2C) which involve a business entity and end consumer, or business-to-government (B2G) which involve a business entity and government.

The volume of B2B transactions is much higher than the volume of B2C transactions. The primary reason for this is that in a typical supply chain there will be many B2B transactions involving subcomponent or raw materials, and only one B2C transaction, specifically sale of the finished product to the end customer.

a. Disruptive technology
b. Customer relationship management
c. Social marketing
d. Business-to-business

14. _____ is one of the four elements of marketing mix. An organization or set of organizations (go-betweens) involved in the process of making a product or service available for use or consumption by a consumer or business user.

The other three parts of the marketing mix are product, pricing, and promotion.

a. Better Living Through Chemistry
b. Japan Advertising Photographers' Association
c. Comparison-Shopping agent
d. Distribution

15. _____ is a broad label that refers to any individuals or households that use goods and services generated within the economy. The concept of a _____ is used in different contexts, so that the usage and significance of the term may vary.

A _____ is a person who uses any product or service.

a. 6-3-5 Brainwriting
b. 180SearchAssistant
c. Power III
d. Consumer

16. _____ is the set of reasons that determines one to engage in a particular behavior. The term is generally used for human _____ but, theoretically, it can be used to describe the causes for animal behavior as well

a. Power III
b. Role playing
c. 180SearchAssistant
d. Motivation

17. _____ is a form of marketing developed from direct response marketing campaigns conducted in the 1970's and 1980's which emphasizes customer retention and satisfaction, rather than a dominant focus on 'point of sale' transactions.

_____ differs from other forms of marketing in that it recognizes the long term value to the firm of keeping customers, as opposed to direct or 'Intrusion' marketing, which focuses upon acquisition of new clients by targeting majority demographics based upon prospective client lists.

_____ refers to long-term and mutually beneficial arrangement wherein both buyer and seller focus on value enhancement through the certain of more satisfying exchange. This approach attempts to transcend the simple purchase exchange process with customer to make more meaningful and richer contact by providing a more holistic, personalized purchase, and use orn consumption experience to create stronger ties.

a. Diversity marketing
b. Global marketing
c. Relationship marketing
d. Guerrilla Marketing

Chapter 2. Building Partnering Relationships

1. _____ is a form of marketing developed from direct response marketing campaigns conducted in the 1970's and 1980's which emphasizes customer retention and satisfaction, rather than a dominant focus on 'point of sale' transactions.

_____ differs from other forms of marketing in that it recognizes the long term value to the firm of keeping customers, as opposed to direct or 'Intrusion' marketing, which focuses upon acquisition of new clients by targeting majority demographics based upon prospective client lists.

_____ refers to long-term and mutually beneficial arrangement wherein both buyer and seller focus on value enhancement through the certain of more satisfying exchange. This approach attempts to transcend the simple purchase exchange process with customer to make more meaningful and richer contact by providing a more holistic, personalized purchase, and use orn consumption experience to create stronger ties.

   a. Global marketing
   b. Guerrilla Marketing
   c. Diversity marketing
   d. Relationship marketing

2. _____ is defined by the American _____ Association as the activity, set of institutions, and processes for creating, communicating, delivering, and exchanging offerings that have value for customers, clients, partners, and society at large. The term developed from the original meaning which referred literally to going to market, as in shopping, or going to a market to sell goods or services.

_____ practice tends to be seen as a creative industry, which includes advertising, distribution and selling.

   a. Product naming
   b. Customer acquisition management
   c. Marketing
   d. Marketing myopia

3. In environmental modeling and especially in hydrology, a _____ model means a model that is acceptably consistent with observed natural processes, i.e. that simulates well, for example, observed river discharge. It is a key concept of the so-called Generalized Likelihood Uncertainty Estimation (GLUE) methodology to quantify how uncertain environmental predictions are.
   a. Behavioral
   b. 6-3-5 Brainwriting
   c. Power III
   d. 180SearchAssistant

Chapter 2. Building Partnering Relationships

4. In marketing, customer _____, lifetime customer value (LCV), or _____ (LTV) and a new concept of 'customer life cycle management' is the present value of the future cash flows attributed to the customer relationship. Use of customer _____ as a marketing metric tends to place greater emphasis on customer service and long-term customer satisfaction, rather than on maximizing short-term sales.

Customer _____ has intuitive appeal as a marketing concept, because in theory it represents exactly how much each customer is worth in monetary terms, and therefore exactly how much a marketing department should be willing to spend to acquire each customer.

   a. Sweepstakes
   b. Brand infiltration
   c. Value chain
   d. Lifetime value

5. A personal and cultural _____ is a relative ethic _____, an assumption upon which implementation can be extrapolated. A _____ system is a set of consistent _____s and measures that is soo not true. A principle _____ is a foundation upon which other _____s and measures of integrity are based.
   a. Supreme Court of the United States
   b. Package-on-Package
   c. Perceptual maps
   d. Value

6. A _____ is a type of business entity in which partners (owners) share with each other the profits or losses of the business undertaking in which all have invested. _____s are often favored over corporations for taxation purposes, as the _____ structure does not generally incur a tax on profits before it is distributed to the partners (i.e. there is no dividend tax levied.) However, depending on the _____ structure and the jurisdiction in which it operates, owners of a _____ may be exposed to greater personal liability than they would as shareholders of a corporation.
   a. Brand piracy
   b. Competition law
   c. Partnership
   d. Fair Debt Collection Practices Act

7. A _____ is a set of companies with interlocking business relationships and shareholdings. It is a type of business group.

The prototypical _____ are those which appeared in Japan during the 'economic miracle' following World War II.

a. Keiretsu
b. 180SearchAssistant
c. 6-3-5 Brainwriting
d. Power III

8. A trade fair (trade show or expo) is an exhibition organized so that companies in a specific industry can showcase and demonstrate their latest products, service, study activities of rivals and examine recent trends and opportunities. Some trade fairs are open to the public, while others can only be attended by company representatives (members of the trade) and members of the press, therefore _____ are classified as either 'Public' or 'Trade Only'. They are held on a continuing basis in virtually all markets and normally attract companies from around the globe.
a. Trade shows
b. 180SearchAssistant
c. Power III
d. 6-3-5 Brainwriting

9. _____ is a contract between two parties, one being the employer and the other being the employee. An employee may be defined as: 'A person in the service of another under any contract of hire, express or implied, oral or written, where the employer has the power or right to control and direct the employee in the material details of how the work is to be performed.' Black's Law Dictionary page 471 (5th ed. 1979.)
a. AMAX
b. ADTECH
c. ACNielsen
d. Employment

10. A supply chain is the system of organizations, people, technology, activities, information and resources involved in moving a product or service from _____ to customer. Supply chain activities transform natural resources, raw materials and components into a finished product that is delivered to the end customer. In sophisticated supply chain systems, used products may re-enter the supply chain at any point where residual value is recyclable.
a. Product line extension
b. Rebate
c. Bringin' Home the Oil
d. Supplier

11. Customer _____ consists of the processes a company uses to track and organize its contacts with its current and prospective customers. CRelationship management software is used to support these processes; information about customers and customer interactions can be entered, stored and accessed by employees in different company departments. Typical CRelationship management goals are to improve services provided to customers, and to use customer contact information for targeted marketing.

Chapter 2. Building Partnering Relationships

a. Green marketing
b. Product bundling
c. Marketing
d. Relationship management

12. _____ is a term developed by Eric von Hippel in 1986. His definition for _____ is:

   1. _____s face needs that will be general in a marketplace - but face them months or years before the bulk of that marketplace encounters them, and
   2. _____s are positioned to benefit significantly by obtaining a solution to those needs.

In other words: _____s are users of a product that currently experience needs still unknown to the public and who also benefit greatly if they obtain a solution to these needs.

The _____ Method is a market research tool that may be used by companies and / or individuals seeking to develop breakthrough products. _____ methodology was originally developed by Dr. Eric von Hippel of the Massachusetts Institute of Technology (MIT) and first described in the July 1986 issue of the Journal of Management Science.

a. Lead user
b. Power III
c. 180SearchAssistant
d. 6-3-5 Brainwriting

13. _____ is a term in economics, where demand for one good or service occurs as a result of demand for another. This may occur as the former is a part of production of the second. For example, demand for coal leads to _____ for mining, as coal must be mined for coal to be consumed.
a. Power III
b. 6-3-5 Brainwriting
c. 180SearchAssistant
d. Derived demand

14. In economics, _____ is the desire to own something and the ability to pay for it. The term _____ signifies the ability or the willingness to buy a particular commodity at a given point of time .

a. Discretionary spending
b. Market system
c. Market dominance
d. Demand

15. Advertising mail junk mail is the delivery of advertising material to recipients of postal mail. The delivery of advertising mail forms a large and growing service for many postal services, and _____ marketing forms a significant portion of the direct marketing industry. Some organizations attempt to help people opt-out of receiving advertising mail, in many cases motivated by a concern over its negative environmental impact.

a. Phishing
b. Directory Harvest Attack
c. Telemarketing
d. Direct mail

16. _____ is the deliberate attempt to manage the public's perception of a subject. The subjects of _____ include people (for example, politicians and performing artists), goods and services, organizations of all kinds, and works of art or entertainment.

From a marketing perspective, _____ is one component of promotion.

a. Brando
b. Publicity
c. Pearson's chi-square
d. Little value placed on potential benefits

Chapter 3. Ethical and Legal Issues in Selling

1. _____ is a branch of philosophy which seeks to address questions about morality, such as how a moral outcome can be achieved in a specific situation (applied _____), how moral values should be determined (normative _____), what moral values people actually abide by (descriptive _____), what the fundamental semantic, ontological, and epistemic nature of _____ or morality is (meta-_____), and how moral capacity or moral agency develops and what its nature is (moral psychology.)

Socrates was one of the first Greek philosophers to encourage both scholars and the common citizen to turn their attention from the outside world to the condition of man. In this view, Knowledge having a bearing on human life was placed highest, all other knowledge being secondary.

   a. ADTECH
   b. AMAX
   c. ACNielsen
   d. Ethics

2. _____ is a form of social influence. It is the process of guiding people toward the adoption of an idea, attitude, or action by rational and symbolic (though not always logical) means. It is strategy of problem-solving relying on 'appeals' rather than coercion.

   a. Power III
   b. 180SearchAssistant
   c. Persuasion
   d. 6-3-5 Brainwriting

3. _____ is the use of governmental powers by government officials for illegitimate private gain. Misuse of government power for other purposes, such as repression of political opponents and general police brutality, is not considered _____. Neither are illegal acts by private persons or corporations not directly involved with the government.

   a. African Americans
   b. Albert Einstein
   c. AStore
   d. Political corruption

4. _____, Gross profit margin or Gross Profit Rate can be defined as the amount of contribution to the business enterprise, after paying for direct-fixed and direct-variable unit costs, required to cover overheads (fixed commitments) and provide a buffer for unknown items. It expresses the relationship between gross profit and sales revenue.

It can be expressed in absolute terms:

Gross Profit = Revenue − Cost of Goods Sold

or as the ratio of gross profit to sales revenue, usually in the form of a percentage:

_____ Percentage = (Revenue-Cost of Goods Sold)/Revenue

Cost of goods sold includes variable costs and fixed costs directly linked to the product, such as material and labor.

   a. Profit maximization
   b. Power III
   c. Gross margin
   d. 180SearchAssistant

5. _____ is an inventory strategy implemented to improve the return on investment of a business by reducing in-process inventory and its associated carrying costs. In order to achieve JIT the process must have signals of what is going on elsewhere within the process. This means that the process is often driven by a series of signals, which can be Kanban , that tell production processes when to make the next part.
   a. Personalization
   b. Promotion
   c. Clutter
   d. Just-in-time

6. _____ is a list for goods and materials held available in stock by a business. It is also used for a list of the contents of a household and for a list for testamentary purposes of the possessions of someone who has died. In accounting _____ is considered an asset.
   a. Ending Inventory
   b. ACNielsen
   c. ADTECH
   d. Inventory

7. _____ or international commercial terms are a series of international sales terms widely used throughout the world. They are used to divide transaction costs and responsibilities between buyer and seller and reflect state-of-the-art transportation practices. They closely correspond to the U.N. Convention on Contracts for the International Sale of Goods.
   a. ADTECH
   b. ACNielsen
   c. International trade
   d. Incoterms

8. _____ as a legal term refers to promotional statements and claims that express subjective rather than objective views, such that no reasonable person would take literally. _____ is especially featured in testimonials.

Chapter 3. Ethical and Legal Issues in Selling

In a legal context, the term originated in the English Court of Appeal case Carlill v Carbolic Smoke Ball Company, which centred on whether a monetary reimbursement should be paid when an influenza preventative device failed to work.

a. Conquesting
b. Custom media
c. Heinz pickle pin
d. Puffery

9. In law, _____ also called calumny, libel for written words, slander for spoken words, is the communication of a statement that makes a claim, expressly stated or implied to be factual, that may give an individual, business, product, group, government or nation a negative image. It is usually, but not always, a requirement that this claim be false and that the publication is communicated to someone other than the person defamed

In common law jurisdictions, slander refers to a malicious, false and defamatory spoken statement or report, while libel refers to any other form of communication such as written words or images.

a. Free good
b. Muckraker
c. Defamation
d. Free trade zone

10. _____ in economics and business is the result of an exchange and from that trade we assign a numerical monetary value to a good, service or asset. If I trade 4 apples for an orange, the _____ of an orange is 4 - apples. Inversely, the _____ of an apple is 1/4 oranges.

a. Discounts and allowances
b. Pricing
c. Contribution margin-based pricing
d. Price

11. _____ exists when sales of identical goods or services are transacted at different prices from the same provider. In a theoretical market with perfect information, no transaction costs or prohibition on secondary exchange (or re-selling) to prevent arbitrage, _____ can only be a feature of monopoly and oligopoly markets, where market power can be exercised. Otherwise, the moment the seller tries to sell the same good at different prices, the buyer at the lower price can arbitrage by selling to the consumer buying at the higher price but with a tiny discount.

a. Penetration pricing
b. Price
c. Resale price maintenance
d. Price discrimination

12. The business terms _____ and pull originated in the logistic and supply chain management, but are also widely used in marketing.

A _____-pull-system in business describes the move of a product or information between two subjects. On markets the consumers usually 'pulls' the goods or information they demand for their needs, while the offerers or suppliers '_____es' them toward the consumers.

a. Gold Key Matching Service
b. Manufacturers' representatives
c. Completely randomized designs
d. Push

13. _____ is the practice whereby a manufacturer and its distributors agree that the latter will sell the former's product at certain prices (_____), at or above a price floor (minimum _____) or at or below a price ceiling (maximum _____.) These rules prevent resellers from competing too fiercely on price and thus driving down profits. Some argue that the manufacturer may do this because it wishes to keep resellers profitable, and thus keeping the manufacturer profitable.
a. Price discrimination
b. Break even analysis
c. Price skimming
d. Resale price maintenance

14. _____ is anything that is generally accepted as payment for goods and services and repayment of debts. The main uses of _____ are as a medium of exchange, a unit of account, and a store of value. Some authors explicitly require _____ to be a standard of deferred payment.
a. Leading indicator
b. Microeconomics
c. Money
d. Law of supply

Chapter 3. Ethical and Legal Issues in Selling

15. Resale _____ is the practice whereby a manufacturer and its distributors agree that the latter will sell the former's product at certain prices (resale _____), at or above a price floor (minimum resale _____) or at or below a price ceiling (maximum resale _____.) These rules prevent resellers from competing too fiercely on price and thus drive down profits. Some argue that the manufacturer may do this because it wishes to keep resellers profitable, and thus keeping the manufacturer profitable.
   a. Price maintenance
   b. Pricing
   c. Transfer pricing
   d. Price points

16. _____ is the ability of an individual or group to seclude themselves or information about themselves and thereby reveal themselves selectively. The boundaries and content of what is considered private differ among cultures and individuals, but share basic common themes. _____ is sometimes related to anonymity, the wish to remain unnoticed or unidentified in the public realm.
   a. Privacy
   b. Power III
   c. 6-3-5 Brainwriting
   d. 180SearchAssistant

17. _____ is the area of law concerned with the protection and preservation of the privacy rights of individuals. Increasingly, governments and other public as well as private organizations collect vast amounts of personal information about individuals for a variety of purposes. The law of privacy regulates the type of information which may be collected and how this information may be used.
   a. Trademark attorney
   b. Privacy law
   c. Collective mark
   d. Madrid system

18. The _____ of 1977 (15 U.S.C. §§ 78dd-1, et seq.) is a United States federal law known primarily for two of its main provisions, one that addresses accounting transparency requirements under the Securities Exchange Act of 1934 and another concerning bribery of foreign officials.
   a. Copyright
   b. Tenth Amendment
   c. Trademark dilution
   d. Foreign Corrupt Practices Act

Chapter 4. Buying Behavior and the Buying Process

1. _____ is an advertisement in which a particular product specifically mentions a competitor by name for the express purpose of showing why the competitor is inferior to the product naming it.

This should not be confused with parody advertisements, where a fictional product is being advertised for the purpose of poking fun at the particular advertisement, nor should it be confused with the use of a coined brand name for the purpose of comparing the product without actually naming an actual competitor. ('Wikipedia tastes better and is less filling than the Encyclopedia Galactica.')

In the 1980s, during what has been referred to as the cola wars, soft-drink manufacturer Pepsi ran a series of advertisements where people, caught on hidden camera, in a blind taste test, chose Pepsi over rival Coca-Cola.

   a. GL-70
   b. Heavy-up
   c. Cost per conversion
   d. Comparative advertising

2. A _____ is a company or individual that purchases goods or services with the intention of reselling them rather than consuming or using them. This is usually done for profit (but could be resold at a loss.) One example can be found in the industry of telecommunications, where companies buy excess amounts of transmission capacity or call time from other carriers and resell it to smaller carriers.
   a. Reseller
   b. Discontinuation
   c. Jobbing house
   d. Value-based pricing

3. _____ is a term in economics, where demand for one good or service occurs as a result of demand for another. This may occur as the former is a part of production of the second. For example, demand for coal leads to _____ for mining, as coal must be mined for coal to be consumed.
   a. Derived demand
   b. 6-3-5 Brainwriting
   c. 180SearchAssistant
   d. Power III

4. _____ is the physical search for minerals, fossils, precious metals or mineral specimens, and is also known as fossicking.

_____ is synonymous in some ways with mineral exploration which is an organised, large scale and at least semi-scientific effort undertaken by mineral resource companies to find commercially viable ore deposits. To actually be considered a prospector you must become registered as a professional prospector.

a. 180SearchAssistant
b. 6-3-5 Brainwriting
c. Power III
d. Prospecting

5. In economics, _____ is the desire to own something and the ability to pay for it. The term _____ signifies the ability or the willingness to buy a particular commodity at a given point of time .

a. Demand
b. Market dominance
c. Market system
d. Discretionary spending

6. A _____, in marketing, procurement, and organizational studies, is a group of employees, family members, or members of any type of organization responsible for purchasing an item for the organization. In a business setting, major purchases typically require input from various parts of the organization, including finance, accounting, purchasing, information technology management, and senior management. Highly technical purchases, such as information systems or production equipment, also require the expertise of technical specialists.

a. Packshot
b. Commercialization
c. Marketing myopia
d. Buying center

7. _____ is systematic determination of merit, worth, and significance of something or someone using criteria against a set of standards. _____ often is used to characterize and appraise subjects of interest in a wide range of human enterprises, including the arts, criminal justice, foundations and non-profit organizations, government, health care, and other human services.

Depending on the topic of interest, there are professional groups which look to the quality and rigor of the _____ process.

a. ADTECH
b. ACNielsen
c. Evaluation
d. AMAX

Chapter 4. Buying Behavior and the Buying Process

8. A personal and cultural _____ is a relative ethic _____, an assumption upon which implementation can be extrapolated. A _____ system is a set of consistent _____s and measures that is soo not true. A principle _____ is a foundation upon which other _____s and measures of integrity are based.
    a. Supreme Court of the United States
    b. Value
    c. Perceptual maps
    d. Package-on-Package

9. _____ is a systematic method to improve the 'value' of goods or products and services by using an examination of function. Value, as defined, is the ratio of function to cost. Value can therefore be increased by either improving the function or reducing the cost.

    a. Power III
    b. Productivity
    c. 180SearchAssistant
    d. Value engineering

10. A _____ or logistics network is the system of organizations, people, technology, activities, information and resources involved in moving a product or service from supplier to customer. _____ activities transform natural resources, raw materials and components into a finished product that is delivered to the end customer. In sophisticated _____ systems, used products may re-enter the _____ at any point where residual value is recyclable.
    a. Purchasing
    b. Supply chain network
    c. Demand chain management
    d. Supply chain

11. _____ refers to a business or organization attempting to acquire goods or services to accomplish the goals of the enterprise. Though there are several organizations that attempt to set standards in the _____ process, processes can vary greatly between organizations. Typically the word '_____' is not used interchangeably with the word 'procurement', since procurement typically includes Expediting, Supplier Quality, and Traffic and Logistics (T'L) in addition to _____.
    a. Drop shipping
    b. Supply chain
    c. Supply network
    d. Purchasing

Chapter 4. Buying Behavior and the Buying Process

12. _____ refers to the structured transmission of data between organizations by electronic means. It is used to transfer electronic documents from one computer system to another (ie) from one trading partner to another trading partner. It is more than mere E-mail; for instance, organizations might replace bills of lading and even checks with appropriate _____ messages.

    a. ADTECH
    b. AMAX
    c. ACNielsen
    d. Electronic data interchange

13. _____ is an inventory strategy implemented to improve the return on investment of a business by reducing in-process inventory and its associated carrying costs. In order to achieve JIT the process must have signals of what is going on elsewhere within the process. This means that the process is often driven by a series of signals, which can be Kanban, that tell production processes when to make the next part.

    a. Clutter
    b. Personalization
    c. Promotion
    d. Just-in-time

14. _____ is a broad label that refers to any individuals or households that use goods and services generated within the economy. The concept of a _____ is used in different contexts, so that the usage and significance of the term may vary.

    A _____ is a person who uses any product or service.

    a. 180SearchAssistant
    b. Consumer
    c. 6-3-5 Brainwriting
    d. Power III

15. _____ refer to a collection of facts usually collected as the result of experience, observation or experiment or a set of premises. This may consist of numbers, words particularly as measurements or observations of a set of variables. _____ are often viewed as a lowest level of abstraction from which information and knowledge are derived.

    a. Pearson product-moment correlation coefficient
    b. Mean
    c. Sample size
    d. Data

Chapter 4. Buying Behavior and the Buying Process

16. _____ is a list for goods and materials held available in stock by a business. It is also used for a list of the contents of a household and for a list for testamentary purposes of the possessions of someone who has died. In accounting _____ is considered an asset.

 a. Inventory
 b. ACNielsen
 c. Ending Inventory
 d. ADTECH

17. _____ in organizations and public policy is both the organizational process of creating and maintaining a plan; and the psychological process of thinking about the activities required to create a desired goal on some scale. As such, it is a fundamental property of intelligent behavior. This thought process is essential to the creation and refinement of a plan, or integration of it with other plans, that is, it combines forecasting of developments with the preparation of scenarios of how to react to them.

 a. 6-3-5 Brainwriting
 b. Power III
 c. 180SearchAssistant
 d. Planning

18. _____ is a branch of philosophy which seeks to address questions about morality, such as how a moral outcome can be achieved in a specific situation (applied _____), how moral values should be determined (normative _____), what moral values people actually abide by (descriptive _____), what the fundamental semantic, ontological, and epistemic nature of _____ or morality is (meta-_____), and how moral capacity or moral agency develops and what its nature is (moral psychology.)

Socrates was one of the first Greek philosophers to encourage both scholars and the common citizen to turn their attention from the outside world to the condition of man. In this view, Knowledge having a bearing on human life was placed highest, all other knowledge being secondary.

 a. Ethics
 b. ADTECH
 c. ACNielsen
 d. AMAX

19. An _____ is a private network that uses Internet protocols, network connectivity, and possibly the public telecommunication system to securely share part of an organization's information or operations with suppliers, vendors, partners, customers or other businesses. An _____ can be viewed as part of a company's intranet that is extended to users outside the company (e.g.: normally over the Internet.) It has also been described as a 'state of mind' in which the Internet is perceived as a way to do business with a preapproved set of other companies business-to-business (B2B), in isolation from all other Internet users.

a. ACNielsen
b. AMAX
c. Extranet
d. ADTECH

20. A _____ is a tool used in industrial business-to-business procurement. It is a type of auction in which the role of the buyer and seller are reversed, with the primary objective to drive purchase prices downward. In an ordinary auction, buyers compete to obtain a good or service.
a. Fulfillment house
b. Vendor Managed Inventory
c. Materials management
d. Reverse auction

Chapter 5. Using Communication Principles to Build Relationships 23

1. _____ is the reverse of encoding, which is the process of transforming information from one format into another. Information about _____ can be found in the following:

- Digital-to-analog converter, the use of analog circuit for _____ operations
- Code, a rule for converting a piece of information into another form or representation
- Code (cryptography), a method used to transform a message into an obscured form
- _____
- _____ methods, methods in communication theory for _____ codewords sent over a noisy channel
- Digital signal processing, the study of signals in a digital representation and the processing methods of these signals
- Word _____, the use of phonics to decipher print patterns and translate them into the sounds of language
- deCODE genetics

a. 6-3-5 Brainwriting
b. Power III
c. 180SearchAssistant
d. Decoding

2. _____ is a term in economics, where demand for one good or service occurs as a result of demand for another. This may occur as the former is a part of production of the second. For example, demand for coal leads to _____ for mining, as coal must be mined for coal to be consumed.
a. 180SearchAssistant
b. Power III
c. 6-3-5 Brainwriting
d. Derived demand

3. _____ is the process of transforming information from one format into another. The opposite operation is called decoding.

Chapter 5. Using Communication Principles to Build Relationships

There are a number of more specific meanings that apply in certain contexts:

- _____ is a basic perceptual process of interpreting incoming stimuli; technically speaking, it is a complex, multi-stage process of converting relatively objective sensory input (e.g., light, sound) into subjectively meaningful experience.
- A content format is a specific _____ format for converting a specific type of data to information.
- Character _____ is a code that pairs a set of natural language characters (such as an alphabet or syllabary) with a set of something else, such as numbers or electrical pulses.
- Text _____ uses a markup language to tag the structure and other features of a text to facilitate processing by computers.
- Semantics _____ of formal language A in formal language B is a method of representing all terms (e.g. programs or descriptions) of language A using language B.
- Electronic _____ transforms a signal into a code optimized for transmission or storage, generally done with a codec.
- Neural _____ is the way in which information is represented in neurons.
- Memory _____ is the process of converting sensations into memories.
- Encryption transforms information for secrecy.

    a. ACNielsen
    b. AMAX
    c. ADTECH
    d. Encoding

4. In economics, _____ is the desire to own something and the ability to pay for it. The term _____ signifies the ability or the willingness to buy a particular commodity at a given point of time.

    a. Demand
    b. Market system
    c. Market dominance
    d. Discretionary spending

5. _____ is the identity of a group or culture, or of an individual as far as one is influenced by one's belonging to a group or culture. _____ is similar to and has overlaps with, but is not synonymous with, identity politics.

There are modern questions of culture that are transferred into questions of identity.

a. 6-3-5 Brainwriting
b. 180SearchAssistant
c. Power III
d. Cultural identity

6. _____ is difficult to define. For example, in 1952, Alfred Kroeber and Clyde Kluckhohn compiled a list of 164 definitions of '_____' in _____: A Critical Review of Concepts and Definitions. However, the word '_____' is most commonly used in three basic senses:

- excellence of taste in the fine arts and humanities
- an integrated pattern of human knowledge, belief, and behavior that depends upon the capacity for symbolic thought and social learning
- the set of shared attitudes, values, goals, and practices that characterizes an institution, organization or group.

When the concept first emerged in eighteenth- and nineteenth-century Europe, it connoted a process of cultivation or improvement, as in agriculture or horticulture. In the nineteenth century, it came to refer first to the betterment or refinement of the individual, especially through education, and then to the fulfillment of national aspirations or ideals.

a. Culture
b. Albert Einstein
c. AStore
d. African Americans

7. _____ comprises a range of practices used in an organisation to identify, create, represent, distribute and enable adoption of insights and experiences. Such insights and experiences comprise knowledge, either embodied in individuals or embedded in organisational processes or practice. An established discipline since 1991 , _____ includes courses taught in the fields of business administration, information systems, management, and library and information sciences .
a. Power III
b. 180SearchAssistant
c. 6-3-5 Brainwriting
d. Knowledge management

8. _____ describes the situation when output from (or information about the result of) an event or phenomenon in the past will influence the same event/phenomenon in the present or future. When an event is part of a chain of cause-and-effect that forms a circuit or loop, then the event is said to 'feed back' into itself.

_____ is also a synonym for:

- _____ Signal; the information about the initial event that is the basis for subsequent modification of the event.
- _____ Loop; the causal path that leads from the initial generation of the _____ signal to the subsequent modification of the event.

_____ is a mechanism, process or signal that is looped back to control a system within itself. Such a loop is called a _____ loop.

a. Feedback
b. Power III
c. 6-3-5 Brainwriting
d. 180SearchAssistant

1. A _____ is a type of business entity in which partners (owners) share with each other the profits or losses of the business undertaking in which all have invested. _____s are often favored over corporations for taxation purposes, as the _____ structure does not generally incur a tax on profits before it is distributed to the partners (i.e. there is no dividend tax levied.) However, depending on the _____ structure and the jurisdiction in which it operates, owners of a _____ may be exposed to greater personal liability than they would as shareholders of a corporation.
   a. Brand piracy
   b. Competition law
   c. Fair Debt Collection Practices Act
   d. Partnership

Chapter 7. Prospecting

1. A _____ is a type of business entity in which partners (owners) share with each other the profits or losses of the business undertaking in which all have invested. _____s are often favored over corporations for taxation purposes, as the _____ structure does not generally incur a tax on profits before it is distributed to the partners (i.e. there is no dividend tax levied.) However, depending on the _____ structure and the jurisdiction in which it operates, owners of a _____ may be exposed to greater personal liability than they would as shareholders of a corporation.
   a. Competition law
   b. Partnership
   c. Fair Debt Collection Practices Act
   d. Brand piracy

2. _____ was a brand of cigarettes produced by W.D. ' H.O. Wills (part of Imperial Tobacco), launched in 1959 but withdrawn in the early 1960s. The launch was accompanied by a huge television advertising campaign, You're never alone with a _____.
   a. GE matrix
   b. Comparison-Shopping agent
   c. Better Living Through Chemistry
   d. Strand

3. An _____ is a private network that uses Internet protocols, network connectivity, and possibly the public telecommunication system to securely share part of an organization's information or operations with suppliers, vendors, partners, customers or other businesses. An _____ can be viewed as part of a company's intranet that is extended to users outside the company (e.g.: normally over the Internet.) It has also been described as a 'state of mind' in which the Internet is perceived as a way to do business with a preapproved set of other companies business-to-business (B2B), in isolation from all other Internet users.
   a. Extranet
   b. ADTECH
   c. ACNielsen
   d. AMAX

4. A trade fair (trade show or expo) is an exhibition organized so that companies in a specific industry can showcase and demonstrate their latest products, service, study activities of rivals and examine recent trends and opportunities. Some trade fairs are open to the public, while others can only be attended by company representatives (members of the trade) and members of the press, therefore _____ are classified as either 'Public' or 'Trade Only'. They are held on a continuing basis in virtually all markets and normally attract companies from around the globe.
   a. 180SearchAssistant
   b. Power III
   c. 6-3-5 Brainwriting
   d. Trade shows

Chapter 7. Prospecting

5. Merchandising refers to the methods, practices and operations conducted to promote and sustain certain categories of commercial activity. The term is understood to have different specific meanings depending on the context. _____ is a sale goods at a store

In marketing, one of the definitions of merchandising is the practice in which the brand or image from one product or service is used to sell another.

 a. New Media Strategies
 b. Merchandising
 c. Merchandise
 d. Sales promotion

6. The _____ or _____ is used by business and government to classify and measure economic activity in Canada, Mexico and the United States. It has largely replaced the older Standard Industrial Classification system; however, certain government departments and agencies, such as the U.S. Securities and Exchange Commission (SEC), still use the SIC codes.

The _____ numbering system is a six-digit code.

 a. Power III
 b. 180SearchAssistant
 c. 6-3-5 Brainwriting
 d. North American industry classification system

7. An _____ is the manufacturing of a good or service within a category. Although _____ is a broad term for any kind of economic production, in economics and urban planning _____ is a synonym for the secondary sector, which is a type of economic activity involved in the manufacturing of raw materials into goods and products.

There are four key industrial economic sectors: the primary sector, largely raw material extraction industries such as mining and farming; the secondary sector, involving refining, construction, and manufacturing; the tertiary sector, which deals with services (such as law and medicine) and distribution of manufactured goods; and the quaternary sector, a relatively new type of knowledge _____ focusing on technological research, design and development such as computer programming, and biochemistry.

 a. ACNielsen
 b. Industry
 c. AMAX
 d. ADTECH

Chapter 7. Prospecting

8. A _____ is a structured collection of records or data that is stored in a computer system. The structure is achieved by organizing the data according to a _____ model. The model in most common use today is the relational model.
   a. 6-3-5 Brainwriting
   b. 180SearchAssistant
   c. Power III
   d. Database

9. _____ is a form of marketing developed from direct response marketing campaigns conducted in the 1970's and 1980's which emphasizes customer retention and satisfaction, rather than a dominant focus on 'point of sale' transactions.

   _____ differs from other forms of marketing in that it recognizes the long term value to the firm of keeping customers, as opposed to direct or 'Intrusion' marketing, which focuses upon acquisition of new clients by targeting majority demographics based upon prospective client lists.

   _____ refers to long-term and mutually beneficial arrangement wherein both buyer and seller focus on value enhancement through the certain of more satisfying exchange. This approach attempts to transcend the simple purchase exchange process with customer to make more meaningful and richer contact by providing a more holistic, personalized purchase, and use orn consumption experience to create stronger ties.

   a. Relationship marketing
   b. Guerrilla Marketing
   c. Diversity marketing
   d. Global marketing

10. _____ refer to a collection of facts usually collected as the result of experience, observation or experiment or a set of premises. This may consist of numbers, words particularly as measurements or observations of a set of variables. _____ are often viewed as a lowest level of abstraction from which information and knowledge are derived.
    a. Sample size
    b. Data
    c. Pearson product-moment correlation coefficient
    d. Mean

11. _____ is the process of extracting hidden patterns from data. As more data is gathered, with the amount of data doubling every three years, _____ is becoming an increasingly important tool to transform this data into information. It is commonly used in a wide range of profiling practices, such as marketing, surveillance, fraud detection and scientific discovery.

a. 180SearchAssistant
b. Power III
c. Structure mining
d. Data mining

12. _____ is defined by the American _____ Association as the activity, set of institutions, and processes for creating, communicating, delivering, and exchanging offerings that have value for customers, clients, partners, and society at large. The term developed from the original meaning which referred literally to going to market, as in shopping, or going to a market to sell goods or services.

_____ practice tends to be seen as a creative industry, which includes advertising, distribution and selling.

a. Customer acquisition management
b. Product naming
c. Marketing
d. Marketing myopia

13. _____ is the process of approaching prospective customers or clients, typically via telephone, who were not expecting such an interaction. The word 'cold' is used because the person receiving the call is not expecting a call or has not specifically asked to be contacted by a sales person.

Within the United Kingdom, the Privacy and Electronic Communications (EC Directive) Regulations 2003 make it unlawful to transmit an automated recorded message for direct marketing purposes via a telephone, without prior consent of the subscriber.

a. Database marketing
b. Cold calling
c. Power III
d. Direct Marketing Associations

14. _____ is the practice whereby a manufacturer and its distributors agree that the latter will sell the former's product at certain prices (_____), at or above a price floor (minimum _____) or at or below a price ceiling (maximum _____.) These rules prevent resellers from competing too fiercely on price and thus driving down profits. Some argue that the manufacturer may do this because it wishes to keep resellers profitable, and thus keeping the manufacturer profitable.

Chapter 7. Prospecting

   a. Price discrimination
   b. Price skimming
   c. Break even analysis
   d. Resale price maintenance

15. _____ in economics and business is the result of an exchange and from that trade we assign a numerical monetary value to a good, service or asset. If I trade 4 apples for an orange, the _____ of an orange is 4 - apples. Inversely, the _____ of an apple is 1/4 oranges.
   a. Pricing
   b. Price
   c. Contribution margin-based pricing
   d. Discounts and allowances

16. Resale _____ is the practice whereby a manufacturer and its distributors agree that the latter will sell the former's product at certain prices (resale _____), at or above a price floor (minimum resale _____) or at or below a price ceiling (maximum resale _____.) These rules prevent resellers from competing too fiercely on price and thus drive down profits. Some argue that the manufacturer may do this because it wishes to keep resellers profitable, and thus keeping the manufacturer profitable.
   a. Pricing
   b. Transfer pricing
   c. Price points
   d. Price maintenance

17. _____ is a method of direct marketing in which a salesperson solicits to prospective customers to buy products or services, either over the phone or through a subsequent face to face or Web conferencing appointment scheduled during the call.

_____ can also include recorded sales pitches programmed to be played over the phone via automatic dialing. _____ has come under fire in recent years, being viewed as an annoyance by many.

   a. Telemarketing
   b. Joe job
   c. Directory Harvest Attack
   d. Phishing

Chapter 8. Planning the Sales Call 33

1. _____ in organizations and public policy is both the organizational process of creating and maintaining a plan; and the psychological process of thinking about the activities required to create a desired goal on some scale. As such, it is a fundamental property of intelligent behavior. This thought process is essential to the creation and refinement of a plan, or integration of it with other plans, that is, it combines forecasting of developments with the preparation of scenarios of how to react to them.
   a. 6-3-5 Brainwriting
   b. 180SearchAssistant
   c. Power III
   d. Planning

2. _____ consists of the processes a company uses to track and organize its contacts with its current and prospective customers. _____ software is used to support these processes; information about customers and customer interactions can be entered, stored and accessed by employees in different company departments. Typical _____ goals are to improve services provided to customers, and to use customer contact information for targeted marketing.
   a. Commercialization
   b. Customer relationship management
   c. Demand generation
   d. Product bundling

3. Customer _____ consists of the processes a company uses to track and organize its contacts with its current and prospective customers. CRelationship management software is used to support these processes; information about customers and customer interactions can be entered, stored and accessed by employees in different company departments. Typical CRelationship management goals are to improve services provided to customers, and to use customer contact information for targeted marketing.
   a. Product bundling
   b. Marketing
   c. Green marketing
   d. Relationship management

4. A personal and cultural _____ is a relative ethic _____, an assumption upon which implementation can be extrapolated. A _____ system is a set of consistent _____s and measures that is soo not true. A principle _____ is a foundation upon which other _____s and measures of integrity are based.
   a. Perceptual maps
   b. Supreme Court of the United States
   c. Package-on-Package
   d. Value

5. In the field of marketing, a customer _____ consists of the sum total of benefits which a vendor promises that a customer will receive in return for the customer's associated payment (or other value-transfer.)

Put simply, the _____ is what the customer gets for his money.

Accordingly, a customer can evaluate a company's value-proposition on two broad dimensions with multiple subsets:

1. relative performance: what the customer gets from the vendor relative to a competitor's offering;
2. price: which consists of the payment the customer makes to acquire the product or service; plus the access cost

The vendor-company's marketing and sales efforts offer a customer _____; the vendor-company's delivery and customer-service processes then fulfill that value-proposition.

A value-proposition can assist in a firm's marketing strategy, and may guide a business to target a particular market segment.

a. Marketing performance measurement and management
b. Value proposition
c. Relationship management
d. DefCom Australia

Chapter 9. Making the Sales Call

1. _____ is a term that refers both to:

   - a formal discipline used to help appraise, or assess, the case for a project or proposal, which itself is a process known as project appraisal; and
   - an informal approach to making decisions of any kind.

   Under both definitions the process involves, whether explicitly or implicitly, weighing the total expected costs against the total expected benefits of one or more actions in order to choose the best or most profitable option. The formal process is often referred to as either CBA (_____) or BCost-benefit analysis

   A hallmark of CBA is that all benefits and all costs are expressed in money terms, and are adjusted for the time value of money, so that all flows of benefits and flows of project costs over time (which tend to occur at different points in time) are expressed on a common basis in terms of their 'present value.' Closely related, but slightly different, formal techniques include Cost-effectiveness analysis, Economic impact analysis, Fiscal impact analysis and Social Return on Investment(SROI) analysis. The latter builds upon the logic of _____, but differs in that it is explicitly designed to inform the practical decision-making of enterprise managers and investors focused on optimising their social and environmental impacts.

   a. Power III
   b. 180SearchAssistant
   c. Cost-benefit analysis
   d. 6-3-5 Brainwriting

2. In economics, '_____' can refer to any kind of predatory pricing. However, the word is now generally used only in the context of international trade law, where _____ is defined as the act of a manufacturer in one country exporting a product to another country at a price which is either below the price it charges in its home market or is below its costs of production. The term has a negative connotation, but advocates of free markets see '_____' as beneficial for consumers and believe that protectionism to prevent it would have net negative consequences.
   a. Sample sales
   b. Gold Key Matching Service
   c. Hawkers
   d. Dumping

3. A _____ is a plan of action designed to achieve a particular goal.

   _____ is different from tactics. In military terms, tactics is concerned with the conduct of an engagement while _____ is concerned with how different engagements are linked.

a. Power III
b. 180SearchAssistant
c. 6-3-5 Brainwriting
d. Strategy

4. In psychology, philosophy, and the cognitive sciences, _____ is the process of attaining awareness or understanding of sensory information. It is a task far more complex than was imagined in the 1950s and 1960s, when it was predicted that building perceiving machines would take about a decade, a goal which is still very far from fruition. The word _____ comes from the Latin words _____, percepio, meaning 'receiving, collecting, action of taking possession, apprehension with the mind or senses.'

_____ is one of the oldest fields in psychology.

a. Groupthink
b. Power III
c. 180SearchAssistant
d. Perception

Chapter 10. Strengthening the Presentation

1. In promotion and of advertising, a _____ or endorsement consists of a written or spoken statement, sometimes from a person figure, sometimes from a private citizen, extolling the virtue of some product. The term '_____' most commonly applies to the sales-pitches attributed to ordinary citizens, whereas 'endorsement' usually applies to pitches by celebrities. See also Testify, Testimony, for historical context and etymology.
    a. Roll-in
    b. Promotional products
    c. Transpromotional
    d. Testimonial

2. Human beings are also considered to be _____ because they have the ability to change raw materials into valuable _____. The term Human _____ can also be defined as the skills, energies, talents, abilities and knowledge that are used for the production of goods or the rendering of services. While taking into account human beings as _____, the following things have to be kept in mind:

    - The size of the population
    - The capabilities of the individuals in that population

    Many _____ cannot be consumed in their original form. They have to be processed in order to change them into more usable commodities.

    a. 180SearchAssistant
    b. 6-3-5 Brainwriting
    c. Power III
    d. Resources

3. _____ is a term used in business for a short document that summarises a longer report, proposal or group of related reports in such a way that readers can rapidly become acquainted with a large body of material without having to read it all. It will usually contain a brief statement of the problem or proposal covered in the major document(s), background information, concise analysis and main conclusions. It is intended as an aid to decision making by business managers.
    a. ADTECH
    b. ACNielsen
    c. Executive summary
    d. AMAX

4. A _____ is an invitation for suppliers, often through a bidding process, to submit a proposal on a specific commodity or service. A bidding process is one of the best methods for leveraging a company's negotiating ability and purchasing power with suppliers. The _____ process brings structure to the procurement decision and allows the risks and benefits to be identified clearly upfront.

a. Lead generation
b. Request for proposal
c. Sales management
d. Hit rate

5. In grammar, the _____ is the form of an adjective or adverb which denotes the degree or grade by which a person, thing and is used in this context with a subordinating conjunction, such as than, as...as, etc.

The structure of a _____ in English consists normally of the positive form of the adjective or adverb, plus the suffix -er e.g. 'he is taller than his father is', or 'the village is less picturesque than the town nearby'.

a. 180SearchAssistant
b. Comparative
c. Power III
d. 6-3-5 Brainwriting

6. _____ is a term that refers both to:

- a formal discipline used to help appraise, or assess, the case for a project or proposal, which itself is a process known as project appraisal; and
- an informal approach to making decisions of any kind.

Under both definitions the process involves, whether explicitly or implicitly, weighing the total expected costs against the total expected benefits of one or more actions in order to choose the best or most profitable option. The formal process is often referred to as either CBA (_____) or BCost-benefit analysis

A hallmark of CBA is that all benefits and all costs are expressed in money terms, and are adjusted for the time value of money, so that all flows of benefits and flows of project costs over time (which tend to occur at different points in time) are expressed on a common basis in terms of their 'present value.' Closely related, but slightly different, formal techniques include Cost-effectiveness analysis, Economic impact analysis, Fiscal impact analysis and Social Return on Investment(SROI) analysis. The latter builds upon the logic of _____, but differs in that it is explicitly designed to inform the practical decision-making of enterprise managers and investors focused on optimising their social and environmental impacts.

a. 180SearchAssistant
b. 6-3-5 Brainwriting
c. Power III
d. Cost-benefit analysis

Chapter 10. Strengthening the Presentation

7. A personal and cultural _____ is a relative ethic _____, an assumption upon which implementation can be extrapolated. A _____ system is a set of consistent _____s and measures that is soo not true. A principle _____ is a foundation upon which other _____s and measures of integrity are based.
    a. Package-on-Package
    b. Supreme Court of the United States
    c. Value
    d. Perceptual maps

8. _____ is a systematic method to improve the 'value' of goods or products and services by using an examination of function. Value, as defined, is the ratio of function to cost. Value can therefore be increased by either improving the function or reducing the cost.

    a. Power III
    b. Productivity
    c. Value engineering
    d. 180SearchAssistant

9. _____ or economic opportunity loss is the value of the next best alternative forgone as the result of making a decision. _____ analysis is an important part of a company's decision-making processes but is not treated as an actual cost in any financial statement. The next best thing that a person can engage in is referred to as the _____ of doing the best thing and ignoring the next best thing to be done.
    a. ACNielsen
    b. Opportunity cost
    c. AMAX
    d. ADTECH

10. In economics, business, retail, and accounting, a _____ is the value of money that has been used up to produce something, and hence is not available for use anymore. In economics, a _____ is an alternative that is given up as a result of a decision. In business, the _____ may be one of acquisition, in which case the amount of money expended to acquire it is counted as _____.
    a. Fixed costs
    b. Variable cost
    c. Transaction cost
    d. Cost

Chapter 10. Strengthening the Presentation

11. _____ is a list for goods and materials held available in stock by a business. It is also used for a list of the contents of a household and for a list for testamentary purposes of the possessions of someone who has died. In accounting _____ is considered an asset.
   a. ACNielsen
   b. Ending Inventory
   c. Inventory
   d. ADTECH

12. The _____ is an equation that equals the cost of goods sold divided by the average inventory. Average inventory equals beginning inventory plus ending inventory divided by 2.

The formula for _____:

$$\text{Inventory Turnover} = \frac{\text{Cost of Goods Sold}}{\text{Average Inventory}}$$

The formula for average inventory:

$$\text{Average Inventory} = \frac{\text{Beginning inventory} + \text{Ending inventory}}{2}$$

A low turnover rate may point to overstocking, obsolescence, or deficiencies in the product line or marketing effort.

   a. AMAX
   b. Inventory turnover
   c. ACNielsen
   d. ADTECH

13. _____ refers to the structured transmission of data between organizations by electronic means. It is used to transfer electronic documents from one computer system to another (ie) from one trading partner to another trading partner. It is more than mere E-mail; for instance, organizations might replace bills of lading and even checks with appropriate _____ messages.
   a. ADTECH
   b. ACNielsen
   c. AMAX
   d. Electronic data interchange

14. _____ is an inventory strategy implemented to improve the return on investment of a business by reducing in-process inventory and its associated carrying costs. In order to achieve JIT the process must have signals of what is going on elsewhere within the process. This means that the process is often driven by a series of signals, which can be Kanban , that tell production processes when to make the next part.
   a. Personalization
   b. Just-in-time
   c. Clutter
   d. Promotion

15. In economic models, the _____ time frame assumes no fixed factors of production. Firms can enter or leave the marketplace, and the cost (and availability) of land, labor, raw materials, and capital goods can be assumed to vary. In contrast, in the short-run time frame, certain factors are assumed to be fixed, because there is not sufficient time for them to change.
   a. Power III
   b. 180SearchAssistant
   c. 6-3-5 Brainwriting
   d. Long-run

16. _____ is a broad label that refers to any individuals or households that use goods and services generated within the economy. The concept of a _____ is used in different contexts, so that the usage and significance of the term may vary.

A _____ is a person who uses any product or service.

   a. Consumer
   b. Power III
   c. 6-3-5 Brainwriting
   d. 180SearchAssistant

17. _____ refer to a collection of facts usually collected as the result of experience, observation or experiment or a set of premises. This may consist of numbers, words particularly as measurements or observations of a set of variables. _____ are often viewed as a lowest level of abstraction from which information and knowledge are derived.
   a. Data
   b. Mean
   c. Pearson product-moment correlation coefficient
   d. Sample size

18. A _____ is a type of business entity in which partners (owners) share with each other the profits or losses of the business undertaking in which all have invested. _____s are often favored over corporations for taxation purposes, as the _____ structure does not generally incur a tax on profits before it is distributed to the partners (i.e. there is no dividend tax levied.) However, depending on the _____ structure and the jurisdiction in which it operates, owners of a _____ may be exposed to greater personal liability than they would as shareholders of a corporation.

   a. Partnership
   b. Fair Debt Collection Practices Act
   c. Brand piracy
   d. Competition law

1. _____ in economics and business is the result of an exchange and from that trade we assign a numerical monetary value to a good, service or asset. If I trade 4 apples for an orange, the _____ of an orange is 4 - apples. Inversely, the _____ of an apple is 1/4 oranges.
   a. Contribution margin-based pricing
   b. Pricing
   c. Discounts and allowances
   d. Price

Chapter 12. Obtaining Commitment

1. _____ or international commercial terms are a series of international sales terms widely used throughout the world. They are used to divide transaction costs and responsibilities between buyer and seller and reflect state-of-the-art transportation practices. They closely correspond to the U.N. Convention on Contracts for the International Sale of Goods.
   a. Incoterms
   b. ADTECH
   c. ACNielsen
   d. International trade

2. _____ is a form of social influence. It is the process of guiding people toward the adoption of an idea, attitude, or action by rational and symbolic (though not always logical) means. It is strategy of problem-solving relying on 'appeals' rather than coercion.
   a. Power III
   b. 180SearchAssistant
   c. Persuasion
   d. 6-3-5 Brainwriting

3. Merchandising refers to the methods, practices and operations conducted to promote and sustain certain categories of commercial activity. The term is understood to have different specific meanings depending on the context. _____ is a sale goods at a store

In marketing, one of the definitions of merchandising is the practice in which the brand or image from one product or service is used to sell another.

   a. Merchandising
   b. Sales promotion
   c. Merchandise
   d. New Media Strategies

Chapter 13. Formal Negotiating 45

1. _____ is a group creativity technique designed to generate a large number of ideas for the solution of a problem. The method was first popularized in the late 1930s by Alex Faickney Osborn in a book called Applied Imagination. Osborn proposed that groups could double their creative output with _____.
   a. Albert Einstein
   b. African Americans
   c. AStore
   d. Brainstorming

2. _____ in organizations and public policy is both the organizational process of creating and maintaining a plan; and the psychological process of thinking about the activities required to create a desired goal on some scale. As such, it is a fundamental property of intelligent behavior. This thought process is essential to the creation and refinement of a plan, or integration of it with other plans, that is, it combines forecasting of developments with the preparation of scenarios of how to react to them.
   a. 180SearchAssistant
   b. 6-3-5 Brainwriting
   c. Planning
   d. Power III

3. _____ generally refers to a list of all planned expenses and revenues. It is a plan for saving and spending. A _____ is an important concept in microeconomics, which uses a _____ line to illustrate the trade-offs between two or more goods.
   a. Budget
   b. 180SearchAssistant
   c. 6-3-5 Brainwriting
   d. Power III

4. A _____ is a business operated under a contract or license associated with a degree of exclusivity in business within a certain geographical area. For example, sports arenas or public parks may have _____ stands. Many department stores contain numerous _____s operated by other retailers.
   a. Promotion
   b. Gross Margin Return on Inventory Investment
   c. Strict liability
   d. Concession

Chapter 14. After the Sale: Building Long-Term Partnerships

1. A personal and cultural _____ is a relative ethic _____, an assumption upon which implementation can be extrapolated. A _____ system is a set of consistent _____s and measures that is soo not true. A principle _____ is a foundation upon which other _____s and measures of integrity are based.
    a. Package-on-Package
    b. Perceptual maps
    c. Supreme Court of the United States
    d. Value

2. _____ is defined by the Oxford English Dictionary as 'the action or practice of selling among or between established clients, markets, traders, etc.' or 'that of selling an additional product or service to an existing customer'. In practice businesses define _____ in many different ways. Elements that might influence the definition might include: the size of the business, the industry sector it operates within and the financial motivations of those required to define the term.
    a. Service provider
    b. Yield management
    c. Freebie marketing
    d. Cross-selling

3. In economic models, the _____ time frame assumes no fixed factors of production. Firms can enter or leave the marketplace, and the cost (and availability) of land, labor, raw materials, and capital goods can be assumed to vary. In contrast, in the short-run time frame, certain factors are assumed to be fixed, because there is not sufficient time for them to change.
    a. Long-run
    b. 180SearchAssistant
    c. Power III
    d. 6-3-5 Brainwriting

4. A _____ is a type of business entity in which partners (owners) share with each other the profits or losses of the business undertaking in which all have invested. _____s are often favored over corporations for taxation purposes, as the _____ structure does not generally incur a tax on profits before it is distributed to the partners (i.e. there is no dividend tax levied.) However, depending on the _____ structure and the jurisdiction in which it operates, owners of a _____ may be exposed to greater personal liability than they would as shareholders of a corporation.
    a. Partnership
    b. Fair Debt Collection Practices Act
    c. Competition law
    d. Brand piracy

Chapter 14. After the Sale: Building Long-Term Partnerships

5. A supply chain is the system of organizations, people, technology, activities, information and resources involved in moving a product or service from _____ to customer. Supply chain activities transform natural resources, raw materials and components into a finished product that is delivered to the end customer. In sophisticated supply chain systems, used products may re-enter the supply chain at any point where residual value is recyclable.

   a. Bringin' Home the Oil
   b. Rebate
   c. Supplier
   d. Product line extension

6. Organizational culture is not the same as _____. It is wider and deeper concepts, something that an organization 'is' rather than what it 'has' (according to Buchanan and Huczynski.)

   _____ is the total sum of the values, customs, traditions and meanings that make a company unique.

   a. Corporate culture
   b. Cross-functional team
   c. 180SearchAssistant
   d. Power III

7. _____ is difficult to define. For example, in 1952, Alfred Kroeber and Clyde Kluckhohn compiled a list of 164 definitions of '_____' in _____: A Critical Review of Concepts and Definitions. However, the word '_____' is most commonly used in three basic senses:

   - excellence of taste in the fine arts and humanities
   - an integrated pattern of human knowledge, belief, and behavior that depends upon the capacity for symbolic thought and social learning
   - the set of shared attitudes, values, goals, and practices that characterizes an institution, organization or group.

   When the concept first emerged in eighteenth- and nineteenth-century Europe, it connoted a process of cultivation or improvement, as in agriculture or horticulture. In the nineteenth century, it came to refer first to the betterment or refinement of the individual, especially through education, and then to the fulfillment of national aspirations or ideals.

   a. AStore
   b. African Americans
   c. Albert Einstein
   d. Culture

Chapter 15. Managing Your Time and Territory

1. A personal and cultural _____ is a relative ethic _____, an assumption upon which implementation can be extrapolated. A _____ system is a set of consistent _____s and measures that is soo not true. A principle _____ is a foundation upon which other _____s and measures of integrity are based.
   a. Value
   b. Perceptual maps
   c. Supreme Court of the United States
   d. Package-on-Package

2. _____ is the process of comparing the cost, cycle time, productivity, or quality of a specific process or method to another that is widely considered to be an industry standard or best practice. The result is often a business case for making changes in order to make improvements. The term _____ was first used by cobblers to measure ones feet for shoes.
   a. Switching cost
   b. Benchmarking
   c. Business strategy
   d. Strategic group

3. _____ is a term in economics, where demand for one good or service occurs as a result of demand for another. This may occur as the former is a part of production of the second. For example, demand for coal leads to _____ for mining, as coal must be mined for coal to be consumed.
   a. 6-3-5 Brainwriting
   b. Derived demand
   c. Power III
   d. 180SearchAssistant

4. In economics, _____ is the desire to own something and the ability to pay for it. The term _____ signifies the ability or the willingness to buy a particular commodity at a given point of time .

   a. Market dominance
   b. Discretionary spending
   c. Demand
   d. Market system

5. _____ in organizations and public policy is both the organizational process of creating and maintaining a plan; and the psychological process of thinking about the activities required to create a desired goal on some scale. As such, it is a fundamental property of intelligent behavior. This thought process is essential to the creation and refinement of a plan, or integration of it with other plans, that is, it combines forecasting of developments with the preparation of scenarios of how to react to them.

a. 180SearchAssistant
b. Power III
c. 6-3-5 Brainwriting
d. Planning

6. _____s are used in open sentences. For instance, in the formula x + 1 = 5, x is a _____ which represents an 'unknown' number. _____s are often represented by letters of the Roman alphabet, or those of other alphabets, such as Greek, and use other special symbols.
a. Personalization
b. Book of business
c. Variable
d. Quantitative

Chapter 16. Managing within Your Company

1. A _____ is a type of business entity in which partners (owners) share with each other the profits or losses of the business undertaking in which all have invested. _____s are often favored over corporations for taxation purposes, as the _____ structure does not generally incur a tax on profits before it is distributed to the partners (i.e. there is no dividend tax levied.) However, depending on the _____ structure and the jurisdiction in which it operates, owners of a _____ may be exposed to greater personal liability than they would as shareholders of a corporation.
   a. Competition law
   b. Brand piracy
   c. Partnership
   d. Fair Debt Collection Practices Act

2. _____ is the process of estimation in unknown situations. Prediction is a similar, but more general term. Both can refer to estimation of time series, cross-sectional or longitudinal data.
   a. Power III
   b. Forecasting
   c. 6-3-5 Brainwriting
   d. 180SearchAssistant

3. _____, Gross profit margin or Gross Profit Rate can be defined as the amount of contribution to the business enterprise, after paying for direct-fixed and direct-variable unit costs, required to cover overheads (fixed commitments) and provide a buffer for unknown items. It expresses the relationship between gross profit and sales revenue.

It can be expressed in absolute terms:

Gross Profit = Revenue − Cost of Goods Sold

or as the ratio of gross profit to sales revenue, usually in the form of a percentage:

_____ Percentage = (Revenue-Cost of Goods Sold)/Revenue

Cost of goods sold includes variable costs and fixed costs directly linked to the product, such as material and labor.

   a. Power III
   b. Gross margin
   c. 180SearchAssistant
   d. Profit maximization

Chapter 16. Managing within Your Company

4. In economics and sociology, an _____ is any factor (financial or non-financial) that enables or motivates a particular course of action, or counts as a reason for preferring one choice to the alternatives. It is an expectation that encourages people to behave in a certain way. Since human beings are purposeful creatures, the study of _____ structures is central to the study of all economic activity (both in terms of individual decision-making and in terms of co-operation and competition within a larger institutional structure.)
   a. AMAX
   b. Incentive
   c. ACNielsen
   d. ADTECH

5. _____ is a branch of philosophy which seeks to address questions about morality, such as how a moral outcome can be achieved in a specific situation (applied _____), how moral values should be determined (normative _____), what moral values people actually abide by (descriptive _____), what the fundamental semantic, ontological, and epistemic nature of _____ or morality is (meta-_____), and how moral capacity or moral agency develops and what its nature is (moral psychology.)

Socrates was one of the first Greek philosophers to encourage both scholars and the common citizen to turn their attention from the outside world to the condition of man. In this view, Knowledge having a bearing on human life was placed highest, all other knowledge being secondary.

   a. ADTECH
   b. ACNielsen
   c. AMAX
   d. Ethics

6. _____ is the study of the Earth and its lands, features, inhabitants, and phenomena. A literal translation would be 'to describe or write about the Earth'. The first person to use the word '_____' was Eratosthenes.
   a. 6-3-5 Brainwriting
   b. Power III
   c. Geography
   d. 180SearchAssistant

7. _____ is concerned with the provisions and use of accounting information to managers within organizations, to provide them with the basis to make informed business decisions that will allow them to be better equipped in their management and control functions.

In contrast to financial accountancy information, _____ information is:

- usually confidential and used by management, instead of publicly reported;
- forward-looking, instead of historical;
- pragmatically computed using extensive management information systems and internal controls, instead of complying with accounting standards.

This is because of the different emphasis: _____ information is used within an organization, typically for decision-making.

According to the Chartered Institute of Management Accountants (CIManagement accounting), _____ is 'the process of identification, measurement, accumulation, analysis, preparation, interpretation and communication of information used by management to plan, evaluate and control within an entity and to assure appropriate use of and accountability for its Resource (economics)resources. _____ also comprises the preparation of financial reports for non-management groups such as shareholders, creditors, regulatory agencies and tax authorities' (CIManagement accounting Official Terminology.)

a. 180SearchAssistant
b. Management accounting
c. 6-3-5 Brainwriting
d. Power III

8. _____ is the provision of service to customers before, during and after a purchase.

According to Turban et al., '_____ is a series of activities designed to enhance the level of customer satisfaction - that is, the feeling that a product or service has met the customer expectation.'

Its importance varies by product, industry and customer.

a. Facing
b. Customer experience
c. COPC Inc.
d. Customer service

9. _____ is an advertisement in which a particular product specifically mentions a competitor by name for the express purpose of showing why the competitor is inferior to the product naming it.

Chapter 16. Managing within Your Company

This should not be confused with parody advertisements, where a fictional product is being advertised for the purpose of poking fun at the particular advertisement, nor should it be confused with the use of a coined brand name for the purpose of comparing the product without actually naming an actual competitor. ('Wikipedia tastes better and is less filling than the Encyclopedia Galactica.')

In the 1980s, during what has been referred to as the cola wars, soft-drink manufacturer Pepsi ran a series of advertisements where people, caught on hidden camera, in a blind taste test, chose Pepsi over rival Coca-Cola.

a. GL-70
b. Cost per conversion
c. Heavy-up
d. Comparative advertising

Chapter 17. Managing Your Career

1. _____ is a term in economics, where demand for one good or service occurs as a result of demand for another. This may occur as the former is a part of production of the second. For example, demand for coal leads to _____ for mining, as coal must be mined for coal to be consumed.
    a. 180SearchAssistant
    b. Power III
    c. 6-3-5 Brainwriting
    d. Derived demand

2. In economics, _____ is the desire to own something and the ability to pay for it. The term _____ signifies the ability or the willingness to buy a particular commodity at a given point of time .

    a. Discretionary spending
    b. Market dominance
    c. Market system
    d. Demand

ANSWER KEY

Chapter 1
    1. a   2. c   3. d   4. d   5. b   6. d   7. d   8. d   9. d   10. d
    11. d   12. a   13. d   14. d   15. d   16. d   17. c

Chapter 2
    1. d   2. c   3. a   4. d   5. d   6. c   7. a   8. a   9. d   10. d
    11. d   12. a   13. d   14. d   15. d   16. b

Chapter 3
    1. d   2. c   3. d   4. c   5. d   6. d   7. d   8. d   9. c   10. d
    11. d   12. d   13. d   14. c   15. a   16. a   17. b   18. d

Chapter 4
    1. d   2. a   3. a   4. d   5. a   6. d   7. c   8. b   9. d   10. d
    11. d   12. d   13. d   14. b   15. d   16. a   17. d   18. a   19. c   20. d

Chapter 5
    1. d   2. d   3. d   4. a   5. d   6. a   7. d   8. a

Chapter 6
    1. d

Chapter 7
    1. b   2. d   3. a   4. d   5. c   6. d   7. b   8. d   9. a   10. b
    11. d   12. c   13. b   14. d   15. b   16. d   17. a

Chapter 8
    1. d   2. b   3. d   4. d   5. b

Chapter 9
    1. c   2. d   3. d   4. d

Chapter 10
    1. d   2. d   3. c   4. b   5. b   6. d   7. c   8. c   9. b   10. d
    11. c   12. b   13. d   14. b   15. d   16. a   17. a   18. a

Chapter 11
    1. d

Chapter 12
    1. a   2. c   3. c

Chapter 13
    1. d   2. c   3. a   4. d

Chapter 14
    1. d   2. d   3. a   4. a   5. c   6. a   7. d

Chapter 15
    1. a   2. b   3. b   4. c   5. d   6. c

Chapter 16
    1. c   2. b   3. b   4. b   5. d   6. c   7. b   8. d   9. d

Chapter 17
    1. d   2. d

www.ingramcontent.com/pod-product-compliance
Lightning Source LLC
Chambersburg PA
CBHW081219230426
43666CB00015B/2807